table of contents

XENON INTERNATIONAL SCHOOL OF HAIR DESIGN
HAIR & MAKE-UP: ANGEL D'AGATA
PHOTO: DEYO'S

TRIBECA COLOR CONSTRUCT
HAIR: JAMES
MAKE-UP: HENI
PHOTO: BRIAN ADAMS

XENON INTERNATIONAL
SCHOOL OF HAIR DESIGN
HAIR & MAKE-UP: NATALIE MARSHALL
PHOTO: DEYO'S

WEDDING HAIR.COM
HAIR: GRETCHEN MAURER
PHOTO: GRETCHEN MAURER

TRENDSETS
HAIR: JORDAN HOPE
PHOTO: SHOOTING STARS,ROBERT HOLMES

LADIES & GENTLEMEN SALON & DAY SPA
HAIR & MAKE-UP: BRENDA BROWN
PHOTO: TOM CARSON

ZONE 5
HAIR: MONICA NILES
PHOTO: SHOOTING STARS,ROBERT HOLMES

CLAIBORNES SALON
PHOTO: DANIEL ACRES

TRENDSETS
HAIR: JORDAN HOPE
PHOTO: SHOOTING STARS,
ROBERT HOLMES

PLANET 21
HAIR & MAKE-UP: PLANET 21 ARTISTIC TEAM
PHOTO: TOM CARSON

PLANET SALON
HAIR & MAKE-UP: SUSIE BEAM
PHOTO: TREVOR BOOKER

PLANET 21
HAIR & MAKE-UP: PLANET 21 ARTISTIC TEAM
PHOTO: TOM CARSON

RALPH PAUL SALON
HAIR: MELISSA LEWELLYN
MAKE-UP: ALLISON JOYCE
PHOTO: JOE DUCHARME

WEDDINGHAIR.COM
HAIR: GRETCHEN MAURER
PHOTO: GRETCHEN MAURER

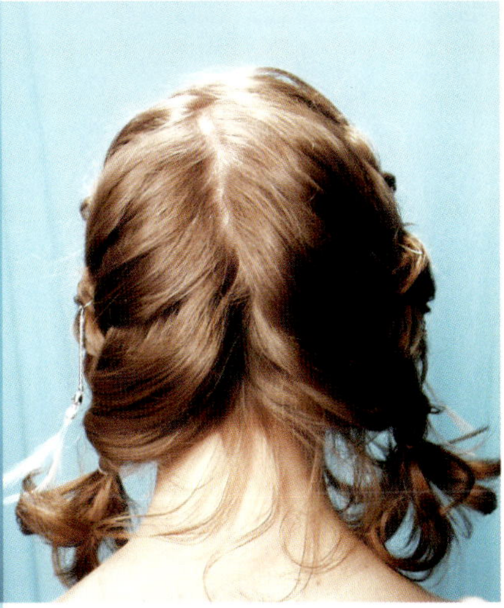

FAIZA AL HARTHY

HAIR BY ANDREA
HAIR: ANDREA CRAWFORD
PHOTO: SHOOTING STARS,ROBERT HOLMES

PLANET 21
HAIR & MAKE-UP: PLANET 21 ARTISTIC TEAM
PHOTO: TOM CARSON

HAIRWORKS
HAIR: JULIE LOVELL
PHOTO: SHOOTING STARS,ROBERT HOLMES

HAIR BY ANDREA
HAIR: ANDREA CRAWFORD
PHOTO: SHOOTING STARS,ROBERT HOLMES

VIS-A-VIS SALON
HAIR: JEFFREY MCQUITHY
MAKE-UP: PAGE SCHNEIDER
PHOTO: TOM CARSON

CLAIBORNE'S SALON
HAIR: DANIEL ACRES

JULIE PETERSON
MAKE-UP: ANGIE KNOST
PHOTO: ANGIE KNOST

PAUL MITCHELL
NATIONAL EDUCATION TEAM
HAIR: DARLENE BURNHAM
MAKE-UP: SHAWN ABRAHAMSON
PHOTO: TOM CARSON

ANGEL HAIR
HAIR: SHARONE
PHOTO: SHOOTING STARS,ROBERT HOLMES

PARAGON SALON
HAIR: KELLI BUTTELWERTH
MAKE-UP: RACHELLE MARGOLEN
PHOTO: SAM VOGEL

MELISSA ANDREW
MAKE-UP: MELISSA ANDREW
PHOTO: ANGIE KNOST

THE A SALON
HAIR: ANDREW RUSSELL
PHOTO: SHOOTING STARS,ROBERT HOLMES

THE NOUVELLE SPA
HAIR: NOUVELLE SPA ARTISTIC TEAM
PHOTO: TOM CARSON

STYLIZED HAIR DESIGN
HAIR: WENDI GREGOIRE
PHOTO: KYRA THAMARUS

JENNIFFER & COMPANY
HAIR & MAKE-UP: CHRISSY KEMP
PHOTO: TOM CARSON

NEW WAVE SALONS
HAIR: CINDY CARRONE
PHOTO: SHOOTING STARS, ROBERT HOLMES

HAIR FX
HAIR: SUZANNE HELLENY
PHOTO: SHOOTING STARS, ROBERT HOLMES

MR. B'S HAIR STUDIO
HAIR: DAVID BLEU
PHOTO: SHOOTING STARS, ROBERT HOLMES

HEADS UP HAIR
HAIR: BRIANA GIBSON
PHOTO: SHOOTING STARS, ROBERT HOLMES

mostly up

LUSH DAY SPA
HAIR: JESSICA TAYLOR
MAKE-UP: TINA ANTIC
PHOTO: SCOTT BRYANT

TRENDSETS
HAIR: JORDAN HOPE
PHOTO: SHOOTING STARS,ROBERT HOLMES

EXPRESSIONS
HAIR: KELLEY COLLINS
PHOTO: SHOOTING STARS, ROBERT HOLMES

HAIR FX
HAIR: SUZANNE HELLENY
PHOTO: SHOOTING STARS, ROBERT HOLMES

mostly up

SALON SANTA FE & SPA
HAIR: JUDITH GROVE
PHOTO: PAMELA GOODMAN

PLANET COLOR
HAIR: JOSEPH M. PACIOREK
MAKE-UP: KATY DURKIN
PHOTO: GARY TRANTAFIL

PLANET COLOR
HAIR: JOSEPH M. PACIOREK
MAKE-UP: KATY DURKIN
PHOTO: GARY TRANTAFIL

MARKFRANK HAIR SALONS
HAIR: ANGIE PIRTLE
MAKE-UP: JANINE SCHIEFELBEIN
PHOTO: JOHN ALVAREZ

DE JENSEN SALON & SPA
HAIR: TARA VOGEL
MAKE-UP: DEBORAH PAOLONE
PHOTO: SCOTT BRYANT

L'IMAGE SALONS
HAIR: KATHERINE DEGROOT
MAKE-UP: TINA LOUDEN
PHOTO: D.MAST

BEST HEAD IN TOWN
HAIR: CARRIE GARRETT
PHOTO: JOSEPH ARMENDARIZ

mostly down

ANGEL HAIR
HAIR: SHARONE
PHOTO: SHOOTING STARS,ROBERT HOLMES

HEADS UP HAIR
HAIR: BRIANA GIBSON
PHOTO: SHOOTING STARS, ROBERT HOLMES

ZONE 5
HAIR: MONICA NILES
PHOTO: SHOOTING STARS,ROBERT HOLMES

TRENDSETS
HAIR: JORDAN HOPE
PHOTO: SHOOTING STARS,ROBERT HOLMES

DE JENSEN SALON & SPA
HAIR & MAKE-UP: DE JENSEN ARTISTIC TEAM
PHOTO: SCOTT BRYANT

TRENDSETS
HAIR: JORDAN HOPE
PHOTO: SHOOTING STARS,ROBERT HOLMES

HAIR DR'S
HAIR: MEG FAULKNER
PHOTO: SHOOTING STARS,ROBERT HOLMES

VICTORIA STATION SALON
HAIR & MAKE-UP: JOCELYN JOHNSON
PHOTO: TOM CARSON

HAIR U WEAR

MICHAEL'S SALON & DAY SPA

L'IMAGE SALONS
HAIR & MAKE-UP: TINA LOUDEN
PHOTO: D. MAST

JENNIFFER & COMPANY
HAIR & MAKE-UP: LISA LAMPERT
PHOTO: TOM CARSON

HAIR U WEAR

HAIR U WEAR

ORLANDO GONZALES
MAKE-UP: DANESSA MYRICKS
DRESS: CASSANDRA JEWELRY: HAIRBOUTIQUE.COM
PHOTO: ERIC VON LOCKHART

BARBARA LHOTAN
MAKE-UP: ILANA HARKAVI
PHOTO: ERIC VON LOCKHART

PIRRI INTERNATIONAL
HAIR: LUIGI PIRRI
MAKE-UP: ARIELLA KEREN
PHOTO: ERIC VON LOCKHART

L'IMAGE SALONS
HAIR & MAKE-UP: TINA LOUDEN
PHOTO: D. MAST

CLIPS SALON & DAY SPA
AIR & MAKE-UP: ECLIPS SALON TEAM
HOTO: SCOTT BRYANT

DETAILS HAIR SALON
HAIR & MAKE-UP: NICOLE FELDT
PHOTO: TOM CARSON

STYLES BY ELIZABETH
HAIR: BETH WILCOX
PHOTO: SHOOTING STARS, ROBERT HOLMES

ESTILO SALON AND DAY SPA
HAIR: DEBBIE COLE
MAKE-UP: ASHLEY ALLISON
PHOTO: BONNIE PENDRAS

DESIGNS BY SANDRA
HAIR: SANDRA RILEY
PHOTO: SHOOTING STARS,ROBERT HOLMES

HAIR DR'S
HAIR & MAKE-UP: MEG FAULKNER
PHOTO: SHOOTING STARS,ROBERT HOLMES

trendy casual

WILLIAM BRETO
MAKE-UP: DIANE SHARP
PHOTO: CAROL SEITZ

THE "A" SALON
HAIR: ANDREW RUSSELL
PHOTO: SHOOTING STARS,ROBERT HOLMES

TRENDSETS
HAIR: JORDAN HOPE
PHOTO: SHOOTING STARS,ROBERT HOLMES

HARRAHS HAIR SKIN & NAILS
HAIR: LUANN HARRAH
MAKE-UP: AMY STALLTER
PHOTO: CHAD MAHLUM

LADIES & GENTLEMEN SALON & DAY SPA
HAIR & MAKE-UP: SANDRA WEIMPERT
PHOTO: TOM CARSON

MANE IMPRESSIONS
HAIR: LAUREN ST. JOHNE
PHOTO: SHOOTING STARS, ROBERT HOLMES

EDIE NOPPENBERGER & SALON TEAM

LADIES & GENTLEMEN SALON & DAY SPA
HAIR: NANCY BROWN
MAKE-UP: SANDRA WEIMPERT
PHOTO: TOM CARSON

STYLES BY JODY
HAIR: JODY KELLEY
PHOTO: SHOOTING STARS,ROBERT HOLMES

HEADS UP HAIR
HAIR: SANDRA KING
PHOTO: SHOOTING STARS,ROBERT HOLMES

NEXXUS

HARRAHS HAIR SKIN & NAILS
HAIR: LUANN HARRAH
MAKE-UP: AMY STALLTER
PHOTO: CHAD MAHLUM

SALON JKL
HAIR: SHARAE U. ARMAND
MAKE-UP: GLENN MOSLEY
PHOTO: TAGGART WINTERHALTER

BARRON'S LONDON SALON
HAIR: DAVID BARRON
MAKE-UP: BARRON'S LONDON SALON
PHOTO: NORMAN ROY

COIFFINA SWITZERLAND

JENNIFFER & COMPANY
HAIR & MAKE-UP: JENNIFER PEALER
PHOTO: TOM CARSON

HARRAHS HAIR SKIN & NAILS
HAIR: LUANN HARRAH
MAKE-UP: AMY STALTER
PHOTO: CHAD MAHLUM

OFF BROADWAY STYLES
HAIR: JAMIE KOONS & TANIA BOUSHELLE
MAKE-UP: BRANDEE BETTENCOURT
PHOTO: SANDY PUC

BOB STEELE HAIRDRESSERS
HAIR: GAVIN STEWART
MAKE-UP: RYAN ANDERSON
PHOTO: TOM CARSON

FRANCESCO'S
HAIR & MAKE-UP: NICOLE WEAVER
PHOTO: TOM CARSON

HUGO SALON
HAIR & MAKE-UP: JESSICA WILSON
PHOTO: HUGO PAEZ

ESTILO SALON AND DAY SPA
HAIR: DEBBIE COLE
MAKE-UP: ASHLEY ALLISON
PHOTO: BONNIE PENDRAS

trendy casual

D.P. & COMPANY
HAIR & MAKE-UP: DALE POTTS
PHOTO: TOM CARSON

FRANCESCO'S COIFFEUR
HAIR: FRANCESCO COLATO
PHOTO: KAREN ROBERTS

KELSEY'S STUDIO FOR HA
HAIR: RICK KELS
MAKE-UP: ANNETTE YANN
PHOTO: JOHN MUS

STYLES BY ELIZABETH
HAIR: ELIZABETH WILCOX
PHOTO: SHOOTING STARS,ROBERT HOLMES

IRY GALLERY
R: GINNY MARONE
OTO: SHOOTING STARS,ROBERT HOLMES

STYLES BY JODY
HAIR: JODY KELLEY
PHOTO: SHOOTING STARS
ROBERT HOLMES

HEADS UP HAIR
HAIR: SANDRA KING
PHOTO: SHOOTING STARS,ROBERT HOLMES

HUGO SALON
HAIR & MAKE-UP: JESSICA WILSON
PHOTO: HUGO PAEZ

ESTILO SALON AND DAY SPA
HAIR: CINDY LANDA
MAKE-UP: ASHLEY ALLISON
PHOTO: BONNIE PENDRAS

classic formal

OFF BROADWAY STYLES
HAIR: LINDA THOMAS
PHOTO: SANDY PUC

NOUFAL HAIRCOLOR STUDIO
HAIR: JOHN ISSA
MAKE-UP: GRETCHEN ALESSI
PHOTO: SCOTT BRYANT

SOUTH CAROLINA ASSOCIATION OF COSMETOLOGY SCHOOLS
HAIR & MAKE-UP: SCACS STUDENTS
PHOTO: CHIP FOUST

L'IMAGE SALONS
HAIR & MAKE-UP: TINA LOUDEN
PHOTO: D. MAST

L'IMAGE SALONS
HAIR: JAMES BURNS
MAKE-UP: MICHAEL FAULK
PHOTO: D. MAST

HARRAHS HAIR SKIN & NAILS
HAIR: LUANN & KREE HARRAH
MAKE-UP: AMY STALLTER
PHOTO: CHAD MAHLUM

NOUVELLE
HAIR & MAKE-UP: NOUVELLE ARTISTIC TEAM
PHOTO: PETER ANTHONY

HAIR FX
HAIR: SUZANNE HELLENY
PHOTO: SHOOTING STARS,ROBERT HOLMES

STYLES BY JODY
HAIR: JODY KELLEY
PHOTO: SHOOTING STARS,ROBERT HOLMES

STYLES BY JODY
HAIR: JODY KELLEY
PHOTO: SHOOTING STARS,ROBERT HOLMES

COIFFINA SWITZERLAND

ESTILO SALON AND DAY SPA
HAIR: CINDY LANDA
MAKE-UP: ASHLEY ALLISON
PHOTO: BONNIE PENDRAS

CURRIE HAIR SKIN-NAILS
HAIR: CHRISTINE RAIMATO
MAKE-UP: ANGELA IARDELLA
PHOTO: TOM CARSON

STYLES BY JODY
HAIR: JODY KELLEY
PHOTO: SHOOTING STARS
ROBERT HOLMES

TRENDSETS
HAIR: JORDAN HOPE
PHOTO: SHOOTING STARS,ROBERT HOLMES

SALON SANTA FE & SPA
HAIR: DONNA KENNEDY
MAKE-UP: DONNA KENNEDY
PHOTO: PAMELA GOODMAN

ESTILO SALON AND DAY SPA
HAIR: LINDA RUDEN
MAKE-UP: ASHLEY ALLISON
PHOTO: BONNIE PENDRAS

LADIES & GENTLEMEN SALON & DAY SPA
HAIR: BONNIE PENDRAS
MAKE-UP: AMY SNYDER
PHOTO: TOM CARSON

L'IMAGE SALONS
HAIR & MAKE-UP: TINA LOUDEN
PHOTO: D. MAST

PLANET COLOR
HAIR: JOSEPH PACIOREK
MAKE-UP: KATY DURKIN
PHOTO: GARY TRANTAFIL

COLLECTIONS SALON & DAY SPA
HAIR: GENOVEVA RODRIGUEZ
MAKE-UP: LINDA LEWIS
PHOTO: KEITH PITTZ

PLANET COLOR
HAIR: JOSEPH PACIOREK
MAKE-UP: KATY DURKIN
PHOTO: GARY TRANTAFIL

BARRON'S LONDON SALON
HAIR: DAVID BARRON
MAKE-UP: BARRON'S LONDON SALON
PHOTO: NORMAN ROY

WILLIAM BRETO
MAKE-UP: DIANE SHARP
PHOTO: CAROL SEITZ

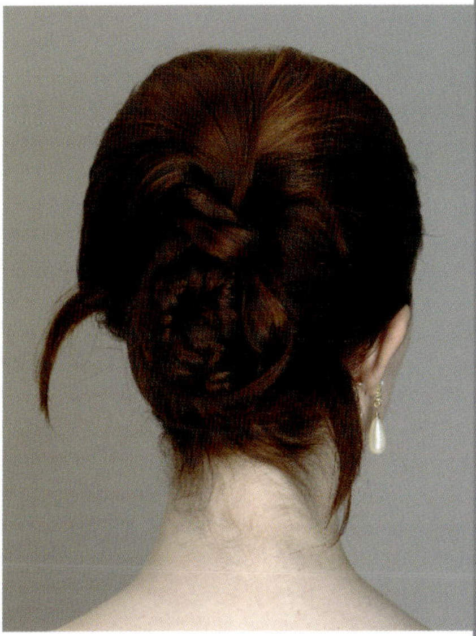

ORLANDO GONZALES
MAKE-UP: DANESSA MYRICKS
DRESS: DI WILLIS DESIGNS
HEADPIECE & JEWELRY: HAIRBOUTIQUE.COM
PHOTO: ERIC VON LOCKHART

HAIR COMES THE BRIDE
HAIR: GINA LUDWIG
MAKE-UP: KATIE CULLUM
PHOTO: BOB ORTIZ

BES REGAL HAIRCOLOR
HAIR: JULIE NEWVILLE
MAKE-UP: ANNA WARK
PHOTO: TOM CARSON

HAIR COMES THE BRIDE
HAIR: GINA LUDWIG
MAKE-UP: KATIE CULLUM
PHOTO: BOB ORTIZ

DE JENSEN SALON & SPA
HAIR: JODIE MCCONNON
MAKE-UP: HEATHER LUBISCHER
PHOTO: SCOTT BRYANT

BARBARA LHOTAN
MAKE-UP: DENESSA MYRICKS
PHOTO: ERIC VON LOCKHART

CURRIE HAIR SKIN-NAILS
HAIR: CARLUCCI COELHO
MAKE-UP: NINA ASADOORIAN
PHOTO: FRANTZ GERMAIN

LAURENCE NUNES
MAKE-UP: DANESSA MYRICKS DRESS: CASSANDRA BROMFIELD PHOTO: ERIC VON LOCKHART

BARBARA LHOTAN
MAKE-UP: DANESSA MYRICKS
DRESS: DESIGNER LOFT   HEADPIECE: LADY DIANNE   JEWELRY: DI WILLIS   PHOTO: ERIC VON LOCKHART

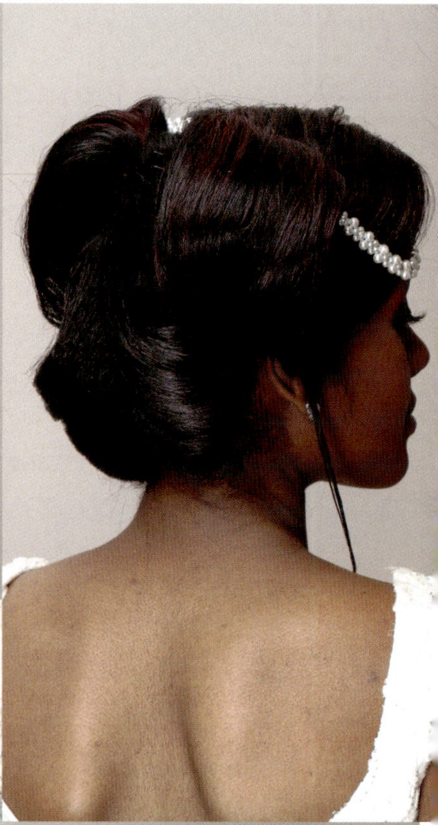

ORLANDO GONZALES
MAKE-UP: DANESSA MYRICKS   DRESS & JEWELRY: DI WILLIS DESIGNS   PHOTO: ERIC VON LOCKHART

BARBARA LHOTAN

MAKE-UP: DANESSA MYRICKS DRESS: DI WILLIS DESIGNS HEADPIECE: ROYAL HATS & HEADPIECES BY LADY DIANNE JEWELRY: DI WILLIS DESIGNS PHOTO: ERIC VON LOCKHART

HAIR INTERNATIONAL
HAIR: KELLY HARDING

HAIR INTERNATIONAL
HAIR: AMANDA HOWARD

HAIR INTERNATIONAL
HAIR: KELLY HARDING

HAIR INTERNATIONAL
HAIR: ELAINE HOLGUIN

HAIR INTERNATIONAL
HAIR: AMANDA HOWARD

WEDDING HAIR.COM
HAIR: GRETCHEN MAURER
MAKE-UP: KRISTINA FORMAN
PHOTO: STEPHEN CIUCCOLI

BARBARA LHOTAN
MAKE-UP: DANESSA MYRICKS DRESS: LUCILLE'S BRIDAL HEADPIECE: AA BRIDAL JEWELRY: HAIRBOUTIQUE.COM
PHOTO: ERIC VON LOCKHART

bridal

WEDDING HAIR.COM
HAIR: GRETCHEN MAURER
MAKE-UP: KRISTINA FORMAN
PHOTO: STEPHEN CIUCCOLI

RANDOLPH'S SALON
HAIR: DANNA CASTILLO
PHOTO: JULIE SWEENY

BARBARA LHOTAN
MAKE-UP: DENESSA MYRICKS
HEADPIECE: HAIRBOUTIQUE.COM
PHOTO: ERIC VON LOCKHART

LADIES & GENTLEMEN SALON & DAY SPA
HAIR & MAKE-UP: ANITA SENSKEY
PHOTO: TOM CARSON

GINA HODGES
PHOTO: ANGIE KNOST

SALON DE CHRISTE
HAIR: BROOKE COY & TAMMY WEIDA
MAKE-UP: CARA WILLIAMS
PHOTO: DAVID SEIDEL

HAIR COMES THE BRIDE
HAIR: GINA LUDWIG
MAKE-UP: KATIE CULLUM
PHOTO: BOB ORTIZ

AXCESS SALON & SPA/DAME ACADEMY
HAIR: ROCCO CAMPANARO
PHOTO: BABAK

BARBARA LHOTAN
MAKE-UP: DANESSA MYRICKS
DRESS: LUCILLE'S BRIDAL
HEADPIECE: HAIRBOUTIQUE.COM
PHOTO: ERIC VON LOCKHART

BARBARA LHOTAN
MAKE-UP: DANESSA MYRICKS DRESS: PAULETTO DESIGNS
HEADPIECE: ROYAL HATS & HEADPIECES BY LADY DIANNE
PHOTO: ERIC VON LOCKHART

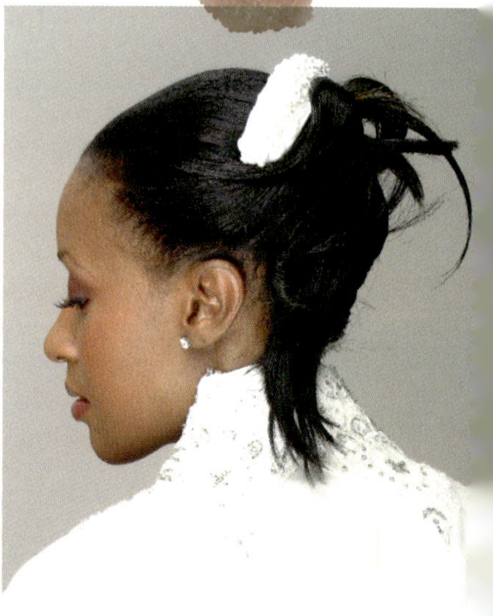

BARBARA LHOTAN
MAKE-UP: DANESSA MYRICKS DRESS: DI WILLIS DESIGNS HEADPIECE: HAIRBOUTIQUE.COM PHOTO: ERIC VON LOCKHART

BARBARA LHOTAN
MAKE-UP: DANESSA MYRICKS DRESS: MANELLI HEADPIECE & JEWELRY: HAIRBOUTIQUE.COM PHOTO: ERIC VON LOCKHART

BARBARA LHOTAN
MAKE-UP: DANESSA MYRICKS DRESS: CASSANDRA BROMFIELD HEADPIECE & JEWELRY: HAIRBOUTIQUE.COM
PHOTO: ERIC VON LOCKHART

BARBARA LHOTAN
MAKE-UP: DANESSA MYRICKS DRESS: CASSANDRA BROMFIELD HEADPIECE & JEWELRY: HAIRBOUTIQUE.COM
PHOTO: ERIC VON LOCKHART

Get Your Work Published!

Receive International Recognition when you're published in INSPIRE

Put your name in the limelight and receive the recognition your hard work deserves. Inspire is the only place to be for worldwide recognition. We are always looking for the latest fresh new looks and styles that are fashionable as well as commercial and are appropriate for salon clientele. We are looking for handsome men and gorgeous women of all ages to portray the latest new looks and trends. No fantasy work please!

Request a Submission Package

All the forms and information you need to submit high quality work in one package. AND, if your work is chosen to be in Inspire you'll receive a complimentary book and press release package as our way of saying thanks.

Call **(800) 634-8500** Email: **inspire@connix.com**
or visit our website at **www.inspirequarterly.com**
to download the forms.

SUBMISSION DEADLINES

- **March 15**
- **June 15**
- **September 15**
- **December 15**

NEW DVD from INSPIRE!

Background Images for Your Salon

Get **Over 240** Background Images to show in your Reception area.

This continous play DVD showcases beautiful hairstyles as a silent background for your Reception area or Front window.

SILENT! 240 Digital Posters played on your DVD player.

ORDER TODAY!

Call 1 800 634-8500

Look for the Special Order form in **THE TECHNICAL: INSIGHTS**

If you are looking for even more hairstyles to choose from...

look for INSPIRE!

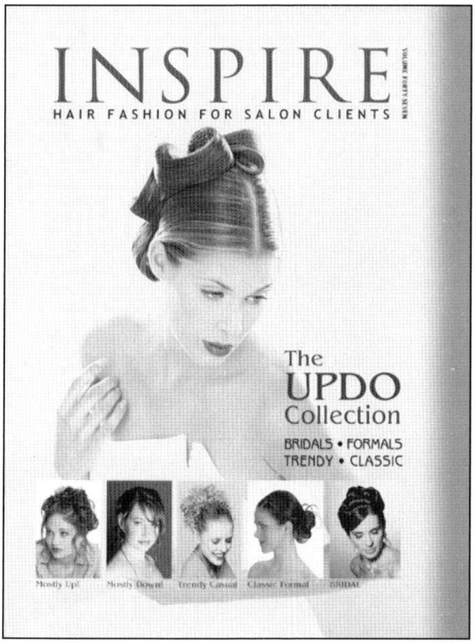

- Hardcover
- 80 Pages
- Full Color Technical
- Easy to Use Sections:

  SHORT
  MEDIUM
  LONG
  Mostly UP!
  Mostly DOWN!
  TRENDY CASUAL
  CLASSIC FORMAL
  BRIDAL

Contact your Distributor TODAY!

In Australia, contact:
Australian International Industries
Unit 7C, Scoresby Industry Park
28 Janine Street, Scoresby
Victoria, 3179, Austalia
CALL: 03-9764-2833
FAX: 03-9764-9709
E-MAIL: admin@aii.net.au

In Brazil, contact:
Escovas Roger
Rua: Mooca, 2112 - Mooca
CEP: 03104-002
Sao Paulo, Brazil
CALL: (5511)6291-6011
FAX: (5511)6692-7465

In Canada, contact:
First Lady Coiffures, Ltd.
14 Mendota Road
Toronto, Canada M8Y 1E8
CALL: 1-800-268-2242
FAX: 416-252-2877
E-MAIL: info@firstladyproducts.com

In Costa Rica, contact:
Mardam M.J. Internacional S.A.
Condominio Las Americas
Planta Baja, San Jose, Costa Rica
CALL: 506-233-6433
FAX: 506-233-6432
E-MAIL: mardammjinternacionalsa@hotmail.com

Ediciones Actuales S.A.
Av 1 Calles 1Y3
Edificio Cristal IV Piso
San Jose, Costa Rica
CALL: 248-1300
E-MAIL: ltecnica@racsa.co.cr

In the Domincan Republic, contact:
Patrocinio International, C. por A.
Ave. 27 de Febrero No. 243
Edificio Yolanda, 2do. Piso Suite 206
Ens. Naco, Santo Domingo
Dominican Republic
CALL: 809-381-0304
FAX: 809-616-2569

In Europe, contact:
Olivia Garden S.A.
Parc Industriel des Hauts Sarts
Rue de Hermee, 255
B-4040 Herstal, Belgium
CALL: 32-4-342-3158
FAX: 32-4-342-3154
E-MAIL: info@oliviagarden.be

In Guatemala, contact:
Sally Beauty Shop
10 Avenida 19-50 Zona
Guatemala
CALL: (502) 333 4873
FAX (502) 333 6170
E-MAILmail: sally@intelnett.com

In Mexico, contact:
Globi De Mexico S.A. De C.V.
Jose Guadalupe Gallo #8640
Colonia Agua Blanca C.P. 45235
Zapopan, Jalisco, Mexico
CALL: (5233)3612-9595
FAX: (5233)3612-9696
E-MAIL: globusman@prodigy.net.mx

In the U.S.A., contact:
Intra America Beauty Network
14 Commerce Drive
North Branford, Connecticut 06471
CALL: 1-800-634-8500
(Tuesday-Friday, between 12:30 & 4:00 EST)
FAX: (203) 484-2118
E-MAIL: inspire@connix.com

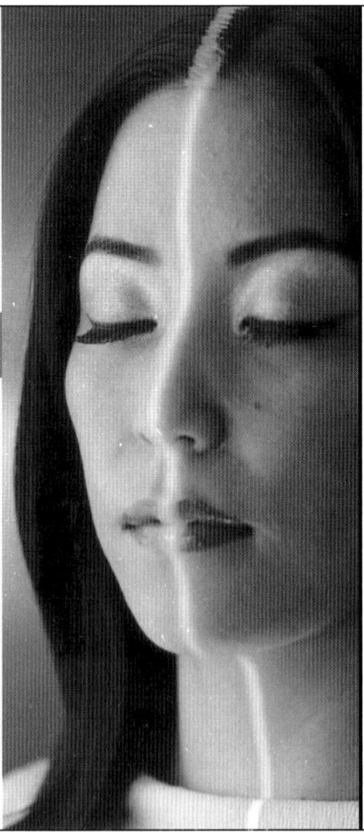